I0500386

Economic Effects of Trout Production by National Fish Hatcheries in the Southeast

Southeast Region, Atlanta, Georgia

Commitment to Fisheries in the Southeast

The importance of the Southeast's fisheries and aquatic resources is clear. These resources are recognized as National assets that contribute to quality of life and well being of the American people. Recreational fishing is deeply woven into the lifestyle and culture of the Southeast. Anglers in the Southeast are the benefactors of many of the contributions that our system of National Fish Hatcheries and Fishery Resource Offices provide. These anglers are often the leaders who fight for improved water quality in our rivers and lakes, better enforcement to prevent overfishing of imperiled stocks, reducing contaminants entering our rivers and streams, restoration of spawning and nursery habitats, and the need to control invasive exotic species entering our waterways. The focus of this report looks at the valuable economic benefits of recreational use of hatchery trout in the Southeast provided by six mitigation fish hatcheries. A significant amount of economic activity is generated as a direct result of trout stocking by National Fish Hatcheries in the Southeast.

I am strongly committed to a viable Fisheries Program in the Southeast Region that will address the needs of our fisheries and aquatic resources for the benefit of the American people. The stakeholders of the Southeast have clearly articulated that a balanced approach is needed that embodies restoration and recovery of imperiled species without abandoning our historic activities that support recreational fishing. I am committed to that approach.

Sam D. Hamilton

Regional Director
Southeast Region
U.S. Fish and Wildlife Service

Executive Summary

■ Trout production and stocking by Federal hatcheries in the southeastern U.S. generates a substantial amount of economic activity for local and regional economies.

■ Six Federal hatcheries in four southeastern States—Arkansas, Kentucky, Tennessee, and Georgia, produce over 6.8 million trout annually and distribute these fish to seven different States in the southeast.

■ Erwin National Fish Hatchery in Tennessee distributes over 11 million eggs annually to both Federal and State hatcheries in over 10 States across the U.S.

■ Recreational angling dependent on the 6 hatcheries generates over $107 million annually in direct expenditures.

■ These expenditures in turn generate over $212 million in related economic activity.

■ Over 2,800 jobs annually are associated with recreational angling dependent on Federal trout production and distribution in the southeastern U.S.

■ These jobs generate earnings of $56 million.

■ Fishing for Federal hatchery trout in the southeastern U.S. results in $1.6 million in State income tax revenue; $5.2 million in State sales tax revenue; and over $5.4 million in Federal income tax revenue. This totals over $12 million in State and Federal tax revenue.

■ Budget expenditures for all six hatcheries total $2.1 million annually.

■ Aggregate consumer surplus or net economic value of angling for Federal hatchery trout in the southeastern U.S. totals almost $51.9 million annually.

■ For each budget dollar spent, recreational trout fishing in the southeastern U.S. generates from $109 to $141 in economic effects.

■ For each budget dollar spent, recreational trout fishing in the southeastern U.S. generates from $5.18 to $7.85 in State and Federal tax revenue.

Introduction

Over the past 120 years, Federal stewardship of the nation's fishery and aquatic resources has been a prime responsibility of the U.S. Fish and Wildlife Service. The Service works with a variety of stakeholders, including Federal agencies, State resource agencies, Tribal governments and private organizations, to improve fishery conservation efforts. This field presence includes: 70 National Fish Hatcheries; 64 Fish and Wildlife Resource Management Offices; nine Fish Health Centers, and six Fish Technology Centers.

The Service focuses its efforts on fulfilling Federal mandates for recovery, restoration, and inter-jurisdictional management of depleted fish stocks. National Fish Hatcheries, Fish and Wildlife Resource Management Offices, Fish Technology Centers and Fish Health Centers focus their efforts to recover aquatic species listed as threatened, endangered or candidates under the Endangered Species Act; restore and maintain depleted anadramous or highly migratory fish stocks and aquatic habitats at productive or self-sustaining levels; and establish, protect or restore resources for which Congress has assigned responsibilities to the Service through legislation (i.e., mitigation of Federal water development projects).

The Service implements several forms of mitigation associated with existing Federal water development projects: 1) minimizing project impacts (i.e. constructing fish-passage facilities); 2) rectifying project impacts (i.e., restoring habitat); and 3) compensating for project impacts (i.e., enhancing fishery resources in reservoirs and tail waters created by Federal water development projects). The fundamental purpose of fishery mitigation is to compensate for adverse impacts to fishery resources caused by the construction of Federal dams and Federal water development projects. Fisheries mitigation in the southeastern U.S. utilizing National Fish Hatcheries consists of stocking trout species (rainbow, brown, brook, lake, and cutthroat trout) in waters impacted by Federal dams.

This report focuses on six mitigation hatcheries in the southeastern U.S.: 1) Greers Ferry NFH, Arkansas; 2) Norfork NFH, Arkansas; 3) Dale Hollow NFH, Tennessee; 4) Erwin NFH, Tennessee; 5) Wolf Creek NFH, Kentucky; and 6) Chattahoochee Forest NFH, Georgia. In their capacity as mitigation hatcheries, these facilities provide a variety of environmental and ecological goods and services. This report focuses on a subset of these goods and services: the economic effects of the recreational use of hatchery trout. Aside from the direct fish-related economic effects, the hatcheries also provide additional economic impacts to local communities and adjacent regions through hatchery budget expenditures, including spending related to trout production and the spending of hatchery staff salaries.

National Fish Hatchery Mitigation in the Southeastern U.S.

Total trout production in the Southeast Region amounts to slightly over 7.5 million fish annually (FY 1999). The vast majority of these fish are produced for mitigation purposes. In the southeastern U.S., fishery mitigation is necessary because the Federal dams on some river systems have drastically altered the environmental conditions of the waters below the dams constructed by the U.S. Army Corps of Engineers (COE) and the Tennessee Valley Authority (TVA). Subsequent to dam construction, the water in the river below the dam is much colder than the river water. This occurs because the water in the river passes through the bottom portion of the dam during the production of electric power. The resulting river water is so cold that fish species like smallmouth bass are not able to survive. Fish species such as rainbow trout were found to be ideally suited to the new coldwater habitat. Because of fluctuating water levels in the rivers associated with sporadic power generation and low flows, limited spawning and reproduction occurs. Tailwaters below Federal dams require mitigation stocking if they are to sustain a fishery. Mitigation hatcheries, as part of the National Fish Hatchery System, compensate for the impacts caused by Federal water development projects. The six hatcheries considered in this report are all mitigation hatcheries, although a given hatchery may have other responsibilities in addition to mitigation.

Greers Ferry NFH
Arkansas

The Greers Ferry NFH is located next to the tail waters of the Greers Ferry Dam (administered by the COE) on the Little Red River, in north central Arkansas. Hatchery construction began in 1965 after the Greers Ferry Dam was completed. The first trout were produced in 1966. Currently, the hatchery produces rainbow and brook trout to mitigate the fishery losses from COE water development projects in central and southeastern Arkansas and eastern Oklahoma. Table 1 shows the annual average distribution of fish releases for the period 1995 to 1999.

About 52 percent of total releases are released into tailwaters or rivers and 46 percent are transferred to other hatcheries. Other hatchery transfers include fingerling trout provided to Federal and State hatcheries involved in fishery mitigation for grow-out purposes. Rainbow trout account for over 93 percent of all releases, while brook trout account for the rest.

Table 2 shows fish distribution by State. Over 87 percent of all fish releases go to Arkansas with the remainder going to Georgia and Oklahoma.

Table 1. Greers Ferry NFH: Fish Distribution Summary Five-year Annual Average (1995-99) *(thousands of fish)*

Species	Tailwater	Reservoirs	Research	To Other Hatcheries	Total
Rainbow	600.8	17.8	15.8	608.2	1,242.6
Brook	84.9	0	0	0	84.9
Total	685.7	17.8	15.8	608.2	1,327.5

Table 2. Greers Ferry NFH: Fish Distribution by State Five-year Annual Average (1995-99) *(thousands of fish)*

Species	Arkansas	Percent of Species Total	Oklahoma	Percent of Species Total	Georgia	Percent of Species Total
Rainbow	1,058.8	86.3%	145.6	11.9%	22.3	1.8%
Brook	84.9	100.0%	0	0%	0	0%
Total	1,143.7	87.2%	145.6	11.1%	22.3	1.7%

Norfork NFH
Arkansas

The Norfork NFH is located below Norfork Dam and Reservoir in Baxter County Arkansas. Authorizing legislation for the Norfolk NFH was based on meeting the fishery needs arising from COE projects in the White River of northern Arkansas and southern Missouri. Table 3 shows Norfolk NFH fish distribution from 1995 to 1999. Rainbow trout comprise about 82 percent of total fish distributed, followed by cutthroat trout at 12 percent and brown trout at 6 percent. The majority of fish are released in tailwaters and rivers (74.3 percent), followed by transfers to other hatcheries

(25.3 percent), reservoirs and lakes (0.3 percent) and research. Other hatchery transfers include fingerling trout provided to Federal and State hatcheries involved in fishery mitigation for grow-out purposes. Rainbows comprise over 82 percent of all releases, followed by cutthroat trout at 11.9 percent and brown trout at 6 percent.

Table 4 shows fish distribution by state. Arkansas receives the vast majority of fish distributed from the Norfork NFH (95.1 percent) while Oklahoma receives about 3.6 percent and Georgia slightly over 1 percent.

Table 3. Norfork NFH:
Fish Distribution Summary
Five-year Annual Average (1995-99)
(thousands of fish)

Species	Tailwater/ Rivers	Reservoirs	Research	To Other Hatcheries	Total
Rainbow	1,175.0	2.5	0.2	445.7	1,623.4
Brown	116.2	3.3	0	0	119.5
Cutthroat	179.4	0	0	55.1	234.5
Total	1,470.6	5.8	0.2	500.8	1,977.4

Table 4. Norfork NFH:
Fish Distribution by State
Five year annual average (1995-99)
(thousands of fish)

Species	Arkansas	Percent of Species Total	Oklahoma	Percent of Species Total	Georgia	Percent of Species Total
Rainbow	1,547.1	95.3%	58.8	3.5%	25.0	1.3%
Brown	111.0	92.9%	8.5	7.1%	0	0%
Cutthroat	234.5	100%	0	0%	0	0%
Total	1,879.6	95.1%	71.1	3.6%	25.0	1.3%

Dale Hollow NFH
Tennessee

Dale Hollow NFH is located in Clay County in north-central Tennessee, just south of the Kentucky border. Dale Hollow's original mission was to mitigate the impacts of Federal water development projects in Tennessee and Kentucky by providing rainbow trout to affected reservoirs, rivers, and tailwaters. The production program has evolved somewhat over the years. The construction of Wolf Creek NFH in

Jamestown, Kentucky in 1975 has enabled Dale Hollow NFH to focus more on needs within Tennessee, Georgia, and Alabama. Current production commitments call for the rearing and distribution of 1.1 million rainbow trout, 200,000 brown trout, and 100,000 lake trout. All of the lake trout and brown trout production as well as the majority of the rainbow trout production (96%) is earmarked for mitigation stocking. Rainbow trout are also provided to the States of Tennessee and Georgia for grow-out on their production facilities. These fish are subsequently stocked into both State and Federal mitigation waters. Rainbow trout are also provided to the Veterans Administration and the Department of Defense for stocking on non-Service lands. All of the non-mitigation fish produced at the Dale Hollow NFH are paid for by the user.

These fish directly support recreational trout fisheries in 64,000 surface acres of impoundment and 115 miles of river/tailwater.

Table 5 shows average annual fish distribution by species for FY 1995-1999. Fish distribution into rivers/tailwaters accounts for 56 percent of total fish distributed, transfers to other hatcheries accounts for 29 percent, fish distribution into reservoirs accounts for 15 percent, and fish utilized for research account for less than 0.01 percent. Rainbow trout account for about 83 percent of all releases, brown trout for 13 percent and lake trout 4 percent.

Table 6 shows fish distribution by state. Overall, Tennessee receives almost 80 percent of total releases, Georgia about 19 percent, Alabama less than 2 percent and Arkansas less than 1 percent.

Table 5. Dale Hollow NFH:
Fish Distribution Summary
5-year Annual Average (1995-99)
(thousands of fish)

Species	Tailwater/ Rivers	Reservoirs	Research	To Other Hatcheries	Total
Rainbow	649.2	164.6	0	419.3	1,233.2
Brown	178.1	1.0	0	13.3	192.4
Lake	0	63.0	0	0	63.0
Total	827.3	228.6	0	432.7	1,488.6

Table 6. Dale Hollow NFH:
Fish Distribution by State
5-year Annual Average (1995-99)
(thousands of fish)

Species	Tennessee	Percent of Species Total	Georgia	Percent of Species Total	Alabama	Percent of Species Total	Arkansas	Percent of Species Total
Rainbow	927.9	75.2%	268.6	21.8%	23.9	1.9%	12.7	1.0%
Brown	179.1	93.1%	13.3	6.9%	0	0%	0	0%
Lake	63.0	100.0%	0	0%	0	0%	0	0%
Total	1,170.0	78.6%	281.9	18.9%	23.9	1.6%	12.7	0.9%

Wolf Creek NFH
Kentucky

Wolf Creek NFH is located in Russell County in south-central Kentucky. The hatchery is situated about 1,800 feet below Wolf Creek Dam. Construction of the 240-foot concrete and earth dam, designed primarily for flood control and hydroelectric generation, was completed in 1950. The resultant impoundment, Lake Cumberland, totals 63,530 surface acres with 1,255 miles of shoreline. Wolf

Creek NFH currently provides mitigation fish for stocking in tailwaters below 13 COE impoundments across six different river basins in Kentucky. That portion of the trout program that takes place on state managed lands is very important to the state of Kentucky. The fish distributed in support of the trout stream program provided over 163 miles of stream fishing in FY 1998. Wolf Creek NFH provided advanced fingerling (6-8 inches) brown trout and catchable (9 inches) rainbow trout in support of ongoing sportfishing programs in 18 state managed lakes and 32 state managed streams in FY 1998. These 50 management areas are located in 43 counties in Kentucky. The hatchery also provides fingerling and advanced fingerling brown trout and advanced fingerling and catchable rainbow trout to the Daniel Boone National Forest in eastern Kentucky. The hatchery

distributes both rainbow and brown trout to two military installations in western Kentucky, Fort Campbell and Fort Knox. Table 7 summarizes fish distribution from 1995 to 1999. Distribution to tailwaters and rivers account for 55 percent of total hatchery distribution; reservoirs and lakes account for 27 percent; transfers to other hatcheries accounts for 17 percent and research accounts for 0.3 percent. Other hatchery transfers include fingerling trout provided to Federal and State hatcheries involved in fishery mitigation for grow-out purposes.

Table 8 shows Wolf Creek NFH fish distribution by state. Kentucky receives most of the releases, accounting for 82 percent, Georgia receives about 9 percent, Tennessee over 6 percent and North Carolina less than 3 percent.

Table 7. Wolf Creek NFH:
Fish Distribution Summary
5-year Annual Average (1995-99)
(thousands of fish)

Species	Tailwater/ Rivers	Reservoirs	Research	To Other Hatcheries	Total
Rainbow	449.7	234.6	2.9	141.9	829.1
Brown	89.9	31.6	0	28.8	150.3
Total	539.6	266.2	2.9	170.7	979.4

Table 8. Wolf Creek NFH:
Fish Distribution by State
5-year Annual Average (1995-99)
(thousands of fish)

Species	Kentucky	Percent of Species Total	Tennessee	Percent of Species Total	Georgia	Percent of Species Total	North Carolina	Percent of Species Total
Rainbow	687.2	82.9%	54.9	6.6%	62.7	7.6%	24.4	2.9%
Brown	114.6	77.2%	9.6	6.5%	24.3	16.4%	0	0%
Total	801.8	82.0%	64.5	6.6%	87.0	8.9%	24.4	2.5%

Chattahoochee Forest NFH
Georgia

The Chattahoochee Forest NFH is located in Fannin County in northern Geogia. It is surrounded by the 750,000 acre Chattahoochee National Forest. The original facility was constructed in 1938 by the Civilian Conservation Corps and was owned and managed by the U.S.

Forest Service and the Bureau of Sport Fisheries. The original purpose of the facility was to conserve, restore and enhance the recreational fisheries on waters within the Chattahoochee National Forest. Brook, brown and rainbow were reared at the hatchery and distributed throughout the streams and lakes of the National Forest. Early production approximated 20,000 fish annually. In 1955, a bilateral agreement between the U.S. Forest Service and the Bureau of Sport Fisheries and Wildlife assigned full responsibility to the Bureau. Production of the facility has been greatly increased through advances in feed and fish culture technology and by upgrading from circular production ponds to raceways. Rainbow trout are the only species currently propagated and presently distribution commitments exceed 900,000 fish annually. The mission of the station has been expanded to

include the mitigation of three Federal water impoundments, providing fish to satisfy obligations of a Memorandum of Understanding (MOU) to the State of Georgia, and providing fish to satisfy the obligations of an MOU with the Eastern Band of Cherokee Indians (North Carolina). Table 9 shows fish distribution from 1995 to 1999. Transfers to other hatcheries accounted for 44 percent of all hatchery releases, tailwater and river stockings accounted for 31.4 percent and the Cherokee MOU accounted for 24 percent. Other hatchery transfers include fingerling trout provided to State hatcheries for grow-out and to the Eastern Band of the Cherokee Indians .

Table 10 shows hatchery fish distribution by state; with Georgia accounting for 76 percent of total fish distributions and North Carolina 24 percent (Tribal fingerling production).

Table 9. Chattahoochee Forest NFH: Fish Distribution Summary 5-year Annual Average (1995-99) (thousands of fish)	Species	Tailwater/ Rivers	Cherokee MOU	To Other Hatcheries	Total
	Rainbow	19.6	82.8%	4.1	17.2%

Table 10. Chattahoochee Forest NFH: Fish Distribution by State 5-year Annual Average (1995-99) (thousands of fish)	Species	Georgia	Percent of Species Total	North Carolina	Percent of Species Total
	Rainbow	785.5	75.9%	250	24.1%

Erwin NFH
Tennessee

The Erwin NFH is located in Unicoi County in Eastern Tennessee near Erwin. It is one of three National Fish Hatcheries rearing rainbow trout in support of the U.S. Fish and Wildlife Service's National Broodstock Program. The hatchery's primary mission is to provide disease-free, eyed trout eggs to the Federal and State hatcheries in the Southeast that rear trout for mitigation stocking. Secondary functions of the hatchery are to provide trout eggs to: 1) fulfill Tribal trust responsibilities for the Eastern Band of Cherokee Indians, according to a Memorandum of Agreement; 2) States for their recreational fishing programs in return for services provided to the FWS; and 3) laboratories needing trout eggs for vital research projects. The egg commitments of the hatchery for all programs range from 10-15 million eyed

eggs annually. These eggs are currently provided by 4 strains of rainbow trout that yield eggs at various times of the year. After the trout are spawned, they are either stocked locally in Tennessee streams and reservoirs or are transferred to other hatcheries in Tennessee, North Carolina, and Virginia. Table 11 shows the distribution of rainbow trout released from Erwin NFH. Transfers to other hatcheries account for 65 percent of all releases, research 15 percent, tailwaters 12 percent and reservoirs 7 percent. Other hatchery transfers include fingerling trout access to numbers needed in developing brood stocks.

Table 12 shows fish distribution by state. Tennessee accounts for over 82 percent of all fish releases and North Carolina accounts for 17 percent.

Table 11. Erwin NFH: Fish Distribution 5-year Annual Average (1995-99) (thousands of fish)	Species	Tailwater/ Rivers	Reservoirs	Research	To Other Hatcheries	Total
	Rainbow	31.4	6.6	6.4	2.0	46.4

Table 12. Erwin NFH: Fish Distribution by State FY 1999 (thousands of fish)	Species	Tennessee	Percent of Species Total	North Carolina	Percent of Species Total
	Rainbow	19.6	82.8%	4.1	17.2%

Economic Effects of Hatchery Mitigation

Federal trout hatcheries provide a variety of environmental and natural resource goods and services. These services can be grouped into three broad categories:

■ Recreation:
- Replacing lost fishing opportunities
- Creating additional fishing opportunities
- Visitor center and facility tours

■ Information:
- Environmental and fisheries educational programs
- Fisheries research
- Fish health diagnostics

■ Federal spending
- Hatchery budget expenditures and their effect on local and regional economies

People who use the above services benefit in the sense that their individual welfare or satisfaction level increases with the use of a particular goods or service. One measure of the magnitude of the change in welfare or satisfaction associated with using a particular good or service is economic value. Aside from the effect on the individual, use of the good or service usually entails spending money in some fashion. These expenditures, in turn, create a variety of economic effects collectively known as economic impacts.

Economic value is the economic trade-off people would be willing to make in order to obtain some good or service. It is the maximum amount people would be willing to pay in order to obtain a particular good or service minus the actual cost of acquisition. In economic theory this is known as net economic value or consumer surplus for more detailed information). In the context of this report, estimates of the economic value of a trout angling day (one person fishing for a portion of one day for trout) are used to determine the aggregate economic value of recreational fishing for trout produced by federal trout hatcheries in the southeastern U.S.

Economic impacts refer to employment, employment income, industrial output and federal and state tax revenue that occur as the result of consumer expenditures on hatchery-related goods and services. For this report, two types of impacts are addressed: 1) impacts associated with annual consumer expenditures on angling for Federally produced trout; and 2) impacts associated with annual hatchery budget expenditures.

A comprehensive economic analysis of Federal trout hatcheries would incorporate estimates of the total societal benefits and costs associated with the hatcheries. For example, benefits would include not only the valuation of trout angling but also the valuation of the scientific knowledge and environmental education services provided by the hatcheries. On the cost side, in addition to annual budget expenditures, the opportunity costs of natural resources such as land and water and the costs of capital improvements would also be included. This report focuses on three types of economic effects: 1) the economic impacts of angler expenditures, which include the effects of angler expenditures on industrial output, employment, employment earning, and Federal and State tax revenue; 2) the economic impacts of hatchery budget expenditures, including both salary and non-salary expenditures and 3) the economic value of recreational trout fishing defined as the net economic value or consumer surplus estimate of a trout angler day.

Economic Impacts of Angler Expenditures

Spending associated with angling can generate a substantial amount of economic activity in local and regional economies. Anglers spend money on a wide variety of goods and services. Trip-related expenditures may include expenses for food, lodging and transportation. Most anglers also buy equipment and angling related goods and services such as rods, reels, lures, hooks, lines, bait, boats, boat fuel, guide and outfitter services, camping equipment, and memberships in fishing clubs and organizations. Because this spending directly affects towns and communities where these purchases are made, angling can have a significant impact on local economies, especially in small towns and rural areas. These direct expenditures are only part of the total picture, however. Businesses and industries that supply the local retailers where the purchases are made also benefit from angler expenditures. For example, a family may decide to purchase a set of fishing rods for an upcoming vacation. Part of the total purchase price will go to the local retailer, say a sporting goods store. The sporting goods store in turn pays a wholesaler who in turn pays the manufacturer of the rods. The manufacturer then spends a portion of this income to cover manufacturing expenses. In this way, each dollar of local retail expenditures can affect a variety of businesses at the local, regional and national level. Consequently, consumer spending associated with angling can have a significant impact on economic activity, employment, household income and local, State and Federal tax revenue. Table 13 shows freshwater angling participation, associated expenditures and economic impacts for the U.S. and the four states in the Southeast Region where the hatcheries addressed in this report are located.

Table 13. Freshwater Angling Effort and related Expenditures, 1996.
(All figures except jobs in millions; jobs in thousands)

Area	Angling Days[2]	Expenditures[3]	Output[4]	Jobs[5]	Earnings[6]
U.S.	485.5	$25,022	$71,508	794.2	$81,502
Arkansas	9.7	$302	$585	9.1	$154
Kentucky	9.6	$517	$1,046	14.1	$267
Tennessee	11.3	$474	$989	12.8	$265
Georgia	12.9	$1,041	$2,122	25.6	$568
State Totals	43.5	$2,334	$4,742	61.6	$1,254

2 Angling day is defined as one person fishing at least part of one day.

3 Includes both travel-related and equipment costs

4 Output is the total value of production or total sales plus or minus inventory (Minnesota IMPLAN Group, Inc., p. 253)

5 Includes both full and part-time employment

6 Earnings are defined as "the earnings that are received by households form the production of regional goods and services and that are available for spending on these goods and services." Thus, earnings are calculated as the sum of wages and salaries, proprietors' income, director's fees, and employer contributions for health insurance less personal contributions for social insurance.

In 1996, U.S. participation in freshwater fishing resulted in over 485 million angler days with over $25 billion in related expenditures. One way to help place these expenditures in context is to think of these expenditures as the annual sales revenue of a company. If such were the case, this company would rank 71st on the 2000 Fortune 500 list, ahead of such companies as Dow Chemical, Microsoft and American Express (Fortune 2001). These expenditures resulted in over $71 billion in industrial output, $18 billion in earnings and almost 800,000 jobs. For the four states where the six National Fish hatcheries are located, freshwater fishing participation amounted to almost 44 million angler days, with associated expenditures of $2.3 billion, industrial output of $4.7 billion, earnings of over $1.2 billion and almost 62,000 jobs.

Estimating the Economic Impacts of Hatchery-Related Angler Expenditures:
To estimate the economic impacts of recreational angling for trout produced by Federal hatcheries, several types of information are needed: 1) the number of State anglers who fish for trout; 2) the annual number of days these anglers fished for trout; and 3) expenditures associated with trout angling. The basic objective is to estimate the Federal trout hatcheries contribution to the overall economic effects of recreational trout fishing in the southeastern U.S.

Number of Trout Anglers:
Information on the number of trout anglers comes from the *1996 National Survey of Fishing, Hunting and Wildlife-Associated Recreation (1996 FHS)* and from State surveys or State information on trout permit sales. Table 14 summarizes the estimated number of trout anglers (both resident and non-resident) by state.

Since the 1996 FHS data matches up fairly well with information provided by State fisheries agencies, the 1996 FHS trout angler data is used in the expenditure and economic output calculations.

Table 14. Annual Number of Trout Anglers by State

State	1996 FHS	State Information	State Source
Kentucky	39,000	36,094	2-yr. average (FY 1999-2000) trout permit holders
Tennessee	120,000	117,000	University of Tennessee
Georgia	160,000	160,000	1996 FHS
Arkansas	152,000	140,000 (1995)	Trout permit holders

Angler Days:

The report *Trout Fishing in the U.S.*, based on the **1996 FHS,** provides estimates of the number of annual trout angler days for each state. Table 15 summarizes data for each state. Also shown for comparison is the annual number of freshwater angling days per angler (freshwater angling includes all freshwater sport fish).

With the exception of Arkansas, the estimates of trout angling days for the other three states are fairly close together, ranging from 9.1 to 10.6 days per year. For all four states, the number of annual freshwater angling days is also fairly close together, ranging from 12.5 to 14.8 days. It is not clear whether the lower number of trout angler days compared with freshwater angler days is an accurate reflection of trout angler behavior or represents an artifact of the methodology or data used to estimate trout angler days. However, since the angler day estimates are tolerably consistent across states and across trout and freshwater anglers (in that trout angler days are consistently lower than freshwater days for all states), trout angler days as noted above will be used in estimating expenditures. This provides, in all likelihood, a reasonable, conservative estimate. However, the estimate of Arkansas trout angler days represents a problem. The 4.2 trout angler days is considerably below the other estimates for the three states and is far below the Arkansas freshwater angler day estimate of 13.1. The Arkansas Game and Fish Commission conducted mail and telephone surveys of trout permit holders in 1988, 1993 and 1999. The most recent information shows that Arkansas trout anglers spent an average of 15.9 days per year fishing for trout. While this number is considerably higher than the trout angler days for the other three states, it is close to the number of freshwater angler days for Arkansas, 13.1. Given the other estimates of trout and freshwater angler days, it seems reasonable to assume that the Arkansas survey estimate of 15.9 days is a more accurate estimate than 4.2 days. Consequently, the Arkansas State trout survey estimate of 15.9 days will be used in estimating expenditures and the resultant economic impacts.

Angler Expenditures:

The expenditures used in this report were obtained from the **1996 FHS.** The expenditures in Table 16 represent statewide averages for freshwater fishing, including both warm and cold-water species. Certain types of equipment purchases, mostly vehicles and boats, are not included. In the actual

Table 15. Annual Number of Trout Angling Days per Angler *(resident and non-resident)*	State	Annual number of **trout** angling days per angler	Annual number of **freshwater** angling days per angler
	Kentucky	10.6	12.5
	Tennessee	9.1	14.8
	Georgia	10.1	13.3
	Arkansas	4.2	13.1

calculations of total angling expenditures associated with each hatchery, expenditures for each State where the fish are caught are used.

It should be noted that these expenditures are on a **per angler per day** basis. The objective in the **1996 FHS** was to obtain information on angling-related expenditures: interviewees were asked about their respective share of trip expenses, not total trip expenses for all members of the party. Consequently, the angling expenditures in the **1996 FHS** represent expenditures of the individual angler; expenditures of non-anglers are not accounted for. While these expenditures are not specific to trout fishing in the southeastern U.S., it is assumed that these expenditures are reasonable, conservative estimates of expenditures associated with trout angling. Few States have conducted an economic analysis of trout fishing and

when they have, the **1996 FHS** has typically been the source of economic data used in the analysis. An exception has been a survey conducted by the Arkansas Game and Fish Commission in 1993 and updated in 1999. Statewide, the survey found that anglers (including both residents and non-residents) spent an average of $194.79 per trip (1993 dollars) for trout fishing. Given that the average trip lasted three days, this gives a per day expenditure total of about $64.93. The **1996 FHS** data show a per day expenditure of $26.61 (1996 dollars). Adjusted for inflation to 1999 dollars, the Arkansas survey figure is $74.73 per day and the **1996 FHS** figure is $28.07 per day. While the Arkansas state survey figure is over twice the **1996 FHS** number, it is not clear if these numbers are exactly comparable since the Arkansas state survey appears to show a per party per day estimate and the **1996 FHS** shows a per angler per day estimate.

Just as the **1996 FHS** expenditure data may undercount non-angler expenditures on fishing trips, the Arkansas state survey may overestimate expenditures. For example, the Arkansas report estimated total state-wide trout angling expenditures by multiplying the total number of trout permit holders in 1993 (129,489) by annual expenditures per trout permit holder (average total fishing trip-related expenditures per trip ($194.79) multiplied by the average number of annual fishing trips taken (5.3) equals $1,032.39). This gives annual expenditures of $133,683,149. Multiplying annual expenditures of trout permit holders by the number of trout permits sold in the state may overstate trout expenditures under certain conditions: 1) the $1,032.39 annual expenditure estimate includes families with more than one trout permit holder, as would be the case, for example, for a family where both the husband and wife hold trout permits. If the $1,032.39

Table 16. Expenditures per Trout Angler per Angling Day *(1999 dollars)*	State	Per angler per day expenditures
	Kentucky	$37.65
	Tennessee	$32.07
	Georgia	$37.02
	Arkansas	$28.07

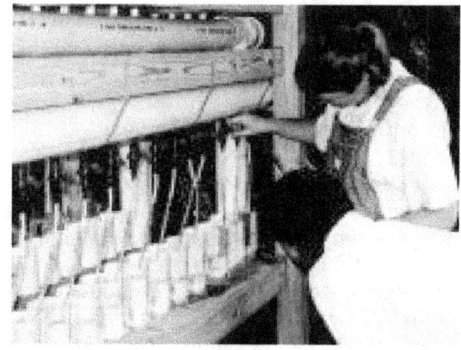

figure represents total annual expenditures for the family as a whole, than multiplying $1,032.39 by the number of trout permit holders in this case, two, results in $2,064.78 in annual expenditures, substantially overstating actual expenditures; 2) the annual expenditure figure includes minors over the age of 15 (in Arkansas, trout permits are required for 16-year olds and above)(Arkansas Game and Fish Commission 2000). Counting a minor trout permit holder who is a member of a family spending $1,032.39 a year on trout angling the same as the adult permit holder(s) for the purpose of calculating total expenditures results in the overestimation of annual expenditures; and 3) if interviewees included expenditures on the non-fishing portion of multipurpose trips in their estimate of fishing trip expenditures.

The purpose of this discussion is not to criticize the two surveys but to account for the rather wide range of the two expenditure estimates. The surveys were done for different purposes using different methodologies and both make a significant contribution in the provision of information on the characteristics of recreational freshwater and trout angling. One approach that may assist in comparing the two estimates is to adjust the Arkansas data to a per angler per day basis. The Arkansas state survey does not contain information on party size; however, a (hopefully) reasonable approach is to assume that party size is

equivalent to household size for the State as a whole and to further assume that all members of the party fish. The most recent (1998) estimate of household size statewide is 2.56 (U.S. Census Bureau 1999). If the per day expenditure total of $74.73 is divided by 2.56, then the per day per person expenditure comes to $29.19 compared with $28.07 for the Arkansas state estimate in the **1996 FHS.** Likewise, if the $74.73 is *per party per day,* multiplying the 1996 FHS *per angler per day* estimate of $28.07 times 2.56 results in a per party per day estimate of $71.86. While the viability of this comparison depends on the reasonableness of assuming that party size and household size are comparable and that all party members fish, it does show that the two estimates may be fairly close when adjusted to be comparable.

For the purposes of this report, angler expenditures from the **1996 FHS** will be used to calculate trout angler expenditures and associated economic impacts with the understanding that the **1996 FHS** expenditures may understate actual expenditures and thus most likely represent a conservative estimate of actual trout angling expenditures.

Method of Estimating National Fish Hatchery Related Expenditures:

Once the basic information components have been identified, it is a relatively straightforward process to calculate trout expenditures which can be attributed to Federal trout hatchery production and releases. The basic approach is as follows: 1) calculate the annual number of trout angler days in each State, 2) determine the proportion of the total number of trout angling days which can be attributed to the Federal trout hatcheries in the State, 3) multiply the estimates in items 1 and 2 above to obtain total annual trout angler days associated with Federal hatcheries in the State, and 4) multiply the estimates obtained in item 3 by the appropriate per day per angler expenditure.

This approach results in an estimate of the total angler expenditures (for a given State) related to fishing for trout produced at Federal trout hatcheries in the southeastern U.S. Determining item 2 above entails two separate estimates: 1) for a given State, the proportion of stocked trout available for recreational angling which can be attributable to Federal trout hatcheries; and 2) the proportion of the total economic effects associated with a hatchery's gross annual production which can be attributed to that hatchery given transfers of trout to other hatcheries. With respect to item 1, estimates were obtained as to the proportion of total trout stocked in a given State attributable to federal trout hatcheries (both as catchables and as transfers to state hatcheries). State fisheries personnel and Federal hatchery managers (need specific sources) provided the following estimates: Kentucky (100%), Arkansas (100%), Georgia (30%), and Tennessee (65%). With respect to item 2, while most Federal trout hatcheries release a majority of their fish as catchables, a significant number of fish are transferred as fingerlings to other hatcheries (both Federal and non-Federal) for further grow-out before being released. It is important to note that expenditures attributable to a specific hatchery have been adjusted to reflect these transfers so that the hatchery only gets credit for its specific contribution to the total grow-out time of the trout eventually released and caught (this is related to item 2 above).

A simple example may help clarify this point. Say the XYZ National Fish Hatchery produces 100 rainbow trout per year. Of this 100, 75 are kept in the Federal hatchery until they reach nine inches, at which time they are released at various stocking points around the State. The remaining 25 are transferred to a State hatchery when 4 1/2 inches; the State hatchery keeps the fish until they reach nine inches and are released. Of the 25 transfers, 50 percent of the total grow-out is attributable to the XYZ

NHF and 50 percent to the State hatchery. Consequently, in determining the angler expenditures attributable to the XYZ NFH, the hatchery receives credit for 75 trout plus 50 percent of the 25 transfers, or 87.5. Consequently, of the total economic effects associated with the 100 released trout, the XYZ NFH gets credit for 87.5 percent.

The estimates obtained from the above approach need to be further adjusted to reflect the proportion of trout angling for wild trout. Tennessee estimates were adjusted to reflect that about 9.8 percent of annual trout angling effort was for wild trout. Georgia estimates were adjusted to reflect that about 33 percent of trout angling effort was for wild trout (Georgia Department of Natural Resources 2000). Kentucky and Arkansas do not have appreciable numbers of wild trout. The above methods are primarily applicable for those States where the southeastern Federal trout hatcheries are located

(Kentucky, Arkansas, Georgia and Tennessee). For other States receiving trout from Federal hatcheries (both catchables and fingerlings), an alternative method was used to calculate trout anglers based on the number of fish released in the State. After trout angler days and adjusted fish releases (to compensate for transfers) were estimated for each hatchery, the ratio of angler days per released fish was calculated. "Angler" days are defined as total trout angler days associated with the adjusted trout releases for a given hatchery. "Released fish" are the total number of trout releases in the state adjusted for transfers to other facilities. Table 18 shows the estimated ratios for the four states where Federal trout hatcheries are located.

These estimates can be used to calculate the number of trout angler days associated with transfers to other States by using the ratio of an adjacent state. For example, the number of trout angler

days associated with transfers to Oklahoma can be estimated using the Arkansas ratio. This assumes that trout angling characteristics and effort are similar in Arkansas and Oklahoma. Using this method, trout angler days associated with transfers to states other than the four above were obtained. The remainder of this report summarizes the economic effects of recreational trout angling attributable to Federal trout hatchery production and stocking. Erwin National Fish Hatchery is not specifically included because of the difficulty in separating out the economic effects attributable to trout egg production and distribution from the economic effects attributable to the released trout. Since all the eggs from the other five Federal hatcheries come from the Erwin National Fish Hatchery, a gross estimate of the economic effects of Erwin NFH egg production and distribution is the aggregate economic effects of the five hatcheries. To this must be added the economic effects of Erwin NFH egg production and distribution to non-Federal hatcheries across the U.S.

Table 17. Trout Angler Days per Released Fish	State	Trout angler day per released fish	Released fish per trout
	Arkansas	0.80	1.25
	Georgia	0.57	1.75
	Tennessee	0.54	1.85
	Kentucky	0.48	2.08

Economic Impacts of Angler Expenditures

Recreational fishing for trout produced and stocked by the various hatcheries results in considerable expenditures for both travel-related goods and services and equipment purchases. Table 18 shows total angler expenditures associated with trout production and distribution for each hatchery along with estimates of the economic output, employment and employment earnings associated with the given expenditures. These estimates were obtained using multipliers from the report, *The Economic Importance of Sport Fishing* published by the American Sportfishing Association (see Appendix A). The multipliers were derived using the Regional Input-Output Modeling System developed by the Bureau of Economic Analysis of the Department of Commerce. The estimated economic impacts in this report are state-wide impacts; information is not available to disaggregate impacts down to the local community or county level.

Total angling expenditures shows the total annual expenditures associated with the recreational catch of the specified hatchery's trout releases. The figures include spending in all states where hatchery fish are released. The different dollar amounts across hatcheries are mainly attributable to four factors: 1) differences in production and release levels; 2) differences in the proportion of total production which is transferred to other hatcheries; 3) differences in the amount of time spent in a Federal hatchery before being transferred; and 4) differences in angler expenditures per angler per day (ranging from $26 to $38 across eight States).

Economic output shows the total industrial output generated by the angler expenditures. Total output is the production value (alternatively, the value of all sales plus or minus inventory) of all output generated by angling expenditures. Total output includes the direct, indirect and induced effects of angling expenditures. Direct effects are simply the initial effects or impacts of spending money; for example, spending money in a grocery store for a fishing trip or purchasing fishing line or bait are examples of direct effects. The purchase of the fishing line by a sporting goods retailer from the line manufacturer or the purchase of canned goods by a grocery from a food wholesaler would be examples of indirect effects. Finally, induced effects refer to the changes in production associated with changes in household income (and spending) caused by changes in employment related to both direct and indirect effects. More simply, people who are employed by the grocery, by the food wholesaler, and by

Table 18. State-wide Economic Impacts Associated with Annual Angling Expenditures, by Hatchery *(dollar figures in thousands, 1999 dollars)*	Hatchery	Total Angling Expenditures	Economic Output	Employment	Employment Earnings
	Dale Hollow TN	$22,714.5	$46,796.2	571	$12,539.9
	Chattahoochee Forest GA	$13,335.2	$25,012.8	286	$6,634.3
	Wolf Creek KY	$16,555.6	$33,357.5	420	$8,549.7
	Norfork AR	$36,858.6	$71,571.8	1,047	$18,838.5
	Greers Ferry AR	$18,366.3	$35,998.2	523	$9,432.1

the line manufacturer spend their income on various goods and services which in turn generate a given level of output. The dollar value of this output is the induced effect of the initial angling expenditures.

The economic impact of a given level of expenditures depends, in part, on the degree of self-sufficiency of the area under consideration. For example, a county with a high degree of self-sufficiency (out-of-county imports are comparatively small) will generally have a higher level of impacts associated with a given level of expenditures than a county with significantly higher imports (a comparatively lower level of self-sufficiency). Consequently, the economic impacts of a given level of expenditures will generally be less for rural and other less economically integrated areas compared with other, more economically diverse areas or regions.

Additionally, the economic impacts estimated in this report are gross state-wide impacts. Information on where expenditures may occur locally and the magnitude of resident and non-resident expenditures (resident and non-resident relative to the geographical area of interest) is not currently available for all the states associated with angling for Federally produced trout. Generally speaking, non-resident expenditures bring "outside" money into the area and thus generate increases in real income or wealth. Spending by residents is simply a transfer of expenditures on one set of goods and services to a different set. In order to calculate "net" economic impacts, much more detailed information would be necessary on expenditure patterns and angler characteristics.

Since this information is not currently available for all the states affected by Federal trout production, gross state-wide estimates are used as an upper-bound for net economic impacts.

Employment and **employment earnings** include direct, indirect and induced effects in a manner similar to total industrial output. Employment includes both full and part-time jobs, with a job defined as one person working for at least part of the calendar year, whether one day or the entire year. **Tax revenues** are shown in Table 19 for State sales tax, State income tax and Federal income tax generated by angler expenditures. Local and county level taxes are not included. Like output, employment and income, tax impacts include direct, indirect and induced tax effects of trout angling expenditures.

Table 19. Tax Revenue Impacts (thousands, 1999 dollars)	Hatchery	State Sales Tax Earnings	State Income Tax	Federal Income Tax	Total Tax Revenue
	Dale Hollow TN	$1,293.5	$66.3	$1,287.6	$2,647.4
	Chattahoochee Forest GA	$497.0	$293.5	$701.8	$1,492.3
	Wolf Creek KY	$959.6	$383.6	$849.1	$2,192.3
	Norfork AR	$1,658.1	$577.7	$1,738.9	$3,974.7
	Greers Ferry AR	$827.2	$274.7	$871.4	$1,973.3

Economic Value of Recreational Trout Angling

Currently there are no available estimates of consumer surplus for trout fishing in the southeastern U.S. Boyle et al. estimate net economic value per (fishing) day for several species of fish in several regions across the U.S. using U.S. Bureau of the Census regions, trout consumer surplus values ranged from $2 to $27 (Pacific, Mountain and Middle Atlantic regions). For U.S. Fish and Wildlife Service trout regions, consumer surplus ranged from $0 to $27 (Western, Mountain and Northeast regions). In lieu of any additional information, it was decided to take the approximate mean of both ranges and use $15 as a reasonable estimate of the net economic value per day of fishing for trout produced by the six federal hatcheries. This $15 figure was then multiplied by total angler days for each hatchery to obtain net economic value shown in Table 20. It is interesting to note that even if consumer surplus were only 76 cents per angling day, this would still result, for each hatchery, in,consumer surplus totals greater than the annual hatchery budget.

Table 20. Net Economic Value of Recreational Trout Angling Associated with Federal Hatcheries

Hatchery	Annual Angler Days	Net Economic Value at $15 per Angling Day
Dale Hollow TN	698,173	$10.5 million
Chattahoochee Forest GA	360,216	$5.4 million
Wolf Creek KY	444,750	$6.7 million
Norfork AR	1,306,035	$19.6 million
Greers Ferry AR	648,327	$9.7 million
Total	3,457,501	$51.9 million

Economic Impacts of Hatchery Budget Expenditures

In addition to angler expenditures, hatchery budget expenditures also contribute to local and regional economies. Table 21 summarizes the economic impacts of both salary and non-salary budget expenditures for each hatchery. Salary expenditures have been reduced by 30 percent to account for taxes, insurance and other deductions. Separate input-output models were used to estimate the impacts of local spending, regional (in-State but not local) and out of State spending for each hatchery for both salary and non-salary budget expenditures. The figures shown for economic output, employment, employment income and tax revenue are aggregate totals for each hatchery across all spending locales. Tax revenue includes local, county, state and federal tax revenue generated by hatchery budget expenditures.

Table 21. Economic Impacts of Hatchery Budget Expenditures *(dollar figures in thousands, 1999 dollars)*

Hatchery	Expenditures	Economic Output	Employment	Employment Income	Tax Revenue
Dale Hollow TN	$422.2	$568.2	7.3	$158.5	$74.9
Chattahoochee Forest GA	$208.8	$297.7	4.1	$84.2	$39.9
Wolf Creek KY	$236.2	$361.5	4.3	$89.5	$43.7
Norfork AR	$589.9	$776.6	9.9	$201.1	$94.6
Greers Ferry AR	$273.0	$391.8	5.3	$99.5	$51.6
Erwin NFH TN	$311.0	$418.6	5.4	$116.8	$55.2
Total	$2,041.0	$2,814.0	36.6	$749.6	$359.9

Summary

Over and above the major contributions of the Federal hatcheries to fisheries conservation in the southeastern U.S., the production and stocking of trout by the six hatcheries results in a significant amount of related economic activity. Table 22 summarizes these effects. Total economic effects (defined here to be economic output plus net economic value) associated with each hatchery range from $30.4 million to over $91.1 million annually. State and Federal tax revenue range from $1.5 million to over $4 million. These totals are far in excess of the annual budgets for each of the hatcheries. The economic effects per $1 of budget expenditure ranges from $109 to $141. Total tax revenue (State and Federal) per $1 of budget expenditure range from $5.18 to $7.85 (note: these figures are not multipliers. They are simply total economic effects divided by the hatchery budget, and total tax revenue divided by the hatchery budget, respectively).

Table 23 shows selected economic indices on a per released fish basis. Again, these are not multipliers but the ratio of the selected variable and the number of fish released annually. In general, comparisons across hatcheries are not valid and should be avoided. Hatcheries have different management objectives and mandates, and consequently differing budgets with which to achieve their respective objectives. Diverse geographic locations result in diverse angling characteristics, effort and expenditures. States have different sales and income tax rates. In addition, the values in Table 23 are *average* values, not *marginal* values. The indices represent a "snap shot" of economic effects based upon current conditions. The indices cannot be used to determine, for example, the economic impact of doubling (or halving) production at any particular hatchery. Nevertheless, these indices may provide a convenient summary statistic based on current conditions and use.

Table 22. Annual Economic Effects Summary for National Fish Hatchery Trout Production (*1999 dollars*)

Hatchery	Total Economic Effects (thousands)	Total State and Federal Tax Revenue Generated (thousands)	Actual Hatchery Budget Expenditures (thousands)	Economic Effects per $1 of Budget Expenditures	Tax Revenue Generated per $1 of Budget Expenditures
Dale Hollow TN	$57,268.8	$2,722.3	$525.8	$109	$5.18
Chattahoochee Forest GA	$30,416.0	$1,532.2	$261.8	$116	$5.85
Wolf Creek KY	$40,028.7	$2,236.0	$284.9	$141	$7.85
Norfork AR	$91,162.3	$4,069.3	$694.4	$131	$5.86
Greers Ferry AR	$45,723.1	$2,024.9	$346.0	$132	$5.85

Table 23. Selected Indices per (*dollars per released fish*)

Hatchery	Angler Expenditures	Economic Value	Tax Revenue	Budget Cost
Dale Hollow TN	$15.26	$7.04	$1.83	$0.36
Chattahoochee Forest GA	$12.88	$5.22	$1.48	$0.25
Wolf Creek KY	$16.90	$6.81	$2.28	$0.29
Norfork AR	$18.64	$9.91	$2.06	$0.35
Greers Ferry AR	$13.84	$7.33	$1.53	$0.26

Appendix A

Multipliers and per Angling Day Economic Impact Indices: The economic impacts associated with angling expenditures for Federally produced trout were estimated using information from a series of reports by Vishwanie Maharaj and Janet Carpenter of the American Sportfishing Association which are summarized in *The Economic Importance of Sport Fishing* published by the American Sportfishing Association (no date). The economic impact estimates were based on freshwater sportfishing expenditures obtained from the *1996 National Survey of Fishing, Hunting, and Wildlife-Associated Recreation.* Table A1 shows economic impacts per $1 of expenditures based on in-state freshwater angling expenditures. Table A2 shows economic impacts per angling day (based on in-state freshwater angling expenditures and total annual freshwater angling days for each state).

Table A1. Economic Impacts per $1 of Sport Fishing Expenditures

State	Output	Earnings	Jobs per $1 million Expenditures	State Sales Tax	State Income Tax	Federal Income Tax
Arkansas	$1.94	$0.51	30.08	$0.045	$0.016	$0.047
Georgia	$1.89	$0.51	22.80	$0.037	$0.023	$0.054
Tennessee	$2.08	$0.56	26.99	$0.060	none	$0.057
Kentucky	$2.02	$0.52	27.24	$0.060	$0.025	$0.051
Oklahoma	$2.06	$0.53	30.15	$0.045	$0.011	$0.049
Mississippi	$1.78	$0.37	22.39	$0.070	$0.008	$0.040
Alabama	$1.97	$0.52	26.45	$0.040	$0.019	$0.052
North Carolina	$1.90	$0.46	22.99	$0.040	$0.019	$0.049

Table A2. Economic Impacts per Freshwater Angling Day

State	Output	Earnings	Jobs per 1,000 Angling Days	State Sales Tax	State Income Tax	Federal Income Tax
Arkansas	$51.53	$13.58	0.80	$1.20	$0.42	$1.25
Georgia	$66.38	$17.79	0.80	$1.31	$0.79	$1.88
Tennessee	$63.35	$16.98	0.82	$1.82	none	$1.74
Kentucky	$72.26	$18.47	0.97	$2.14	$0.87	$1.82
Oklahoma	$57.33	$14.66	0.84	$1.25	$0.31	$1.37
Mississippi	$58.76	$12.27	0.74	$2.31	$0.26	$1.33
Alabama	$61.30	$16.23	0.82	$1.24	$0.60	$1.62
North Carolina	$61.33	$14.82	0.74	$1.29	$0.63	$1.58

Summary of Fish Stocking Locations

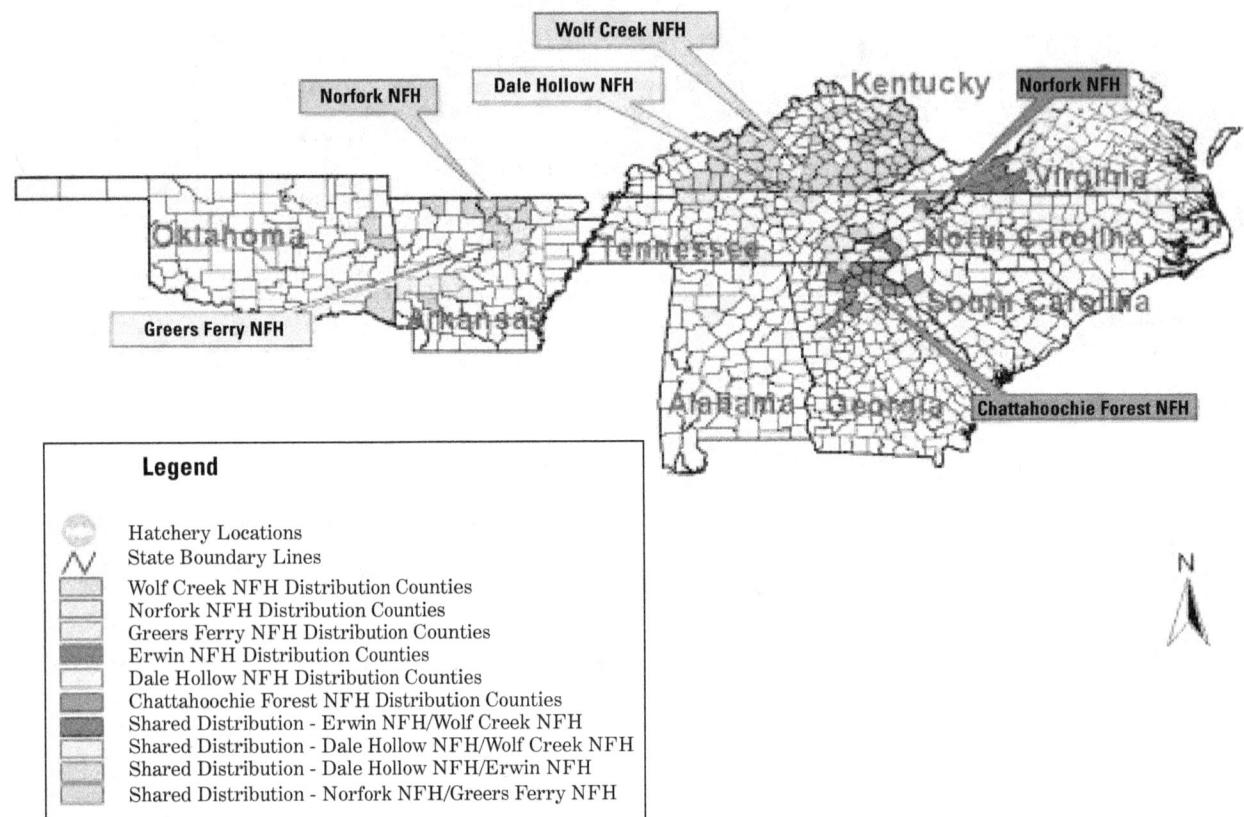

Legend

- ⊙ Hatchery Locations
- ⋀ State Boundary Lines
- Wolf Creek NFH Distribution Counties
- Norfork NFH Distribution Counties
- Greers Ferry NFH Distribution Counties
- Erwin NFH Distribution Counties
- Dale Hollow NFH Distribution Counties
- Chattahoochie Forest NFH Distribution Counties
- Shared Distribution - Erwin NFH/Wolf Creek NFH
- Shared Distribution - Dale Hollow NFH/Wolf Creek NFH
- Shared Distribution - Dale Hollow NFH/Erwin NFH
- Shared Distribution - Norfork NFH/Greers Ferry NFH

N

This map was produced at the GIS Center in the Cookeville, TN Field Office, February 2001